salmonpoetry

Diverse Voices from Ireland and the World

Also by Mary Dorcey

POETRY

Kindling
(Onlywomen Press, 1982)

Moving into the Space Cleared by Our Mothers
(Salmon, 1991)

The River That Carries Me
(Salmon, 1995)

Like Joy in Season, Like Sorrow
(Salmon, 2001)

Perhaps the Heart is Constant After All
(Salmon, 2012)

To Air the Soul, Throw All the Windows Wide: New & Selected Poems
(Salmon, 2016)

FICTION

A Noise from the Woodshed
(Onlywomen Press, 1987)

Scarlet O'Hara, a novella
(Onlywomen Press, 1993)

Biography of Desire
(Poolbeg, 1997)

Life Holds Its Breath

MARY DORCEY

Published in 2022 by
Salmon Poetry
Cliffs of Moher, County Clare, Ireland
Website: www.salmonpoetry.com
Email: info@salmonpoetry.com

Copyright © Mary Dorcey, 2022

ISBN 978-1-915022-04-2

All rights reserved. No part of this publication may be reproduced or transmitted in any form or by any means, electronic or mechanical, including photography, recording, or any information storage or retrieval system, without permission in writing from the publisher. The book is sold subject to the condition that it shall not, by way of trade or otherwise, be lent, resold or otherwise circulated without the publisher's prior consent in any form of binding or cover other than that in which it is published and without a similar condition, including this condition, being imposed on the subsequent purchaser.

Cover Image: *Uisce Anam 'j'* by Janet Pierce, watercolour on paper, 2016
Cover Design & Typesetting: *Siobhán Hutson*

Printed in Ireland by Sprint Print

Salmon Poetry gratefully acknowledges the support of
The Arts Council / An Chomhairle Ealaíon

for Ursula Halligan

CONTENTS

1. *Youth Come Again and Summer*

Do Not Count The Hours	11
The Heart Is Like That	13
Reason Rivals Blood	15
If Our Paths Were To Cross	17
The Forgotten Gift	19
What We Take As Grace	20
After Rain	21
In My House	22
Most Days	23

2. *Life Holds Its Breath*

In Days of Contagion	29
Alarmed By Sudden Warning	32
Another Pastoral	34
Predation of Earth	36
Eden	38

3. *The Artist's Road*

Common Questions And Some Answers	43
Between The Shafts	44
The Painter's Cat	46
Words	48
The Narrow Track, Grief	50
A Last Glimpse Of Summer	52

salmonpoetry
Cliffs of Moher, County Clare, Ireland

"Publishing the finest Irish and international literature."
Michael D. Higgins, President of Ireland

MARY DORCEY is a critically acclaimed Irish poet, short story writer and novelist. She won the Rooney Prize for Irish Literature in 1990 for her short story collection *A Noise from the Woodshed*. Her poetry and fiction is researched and taught internationally at universities throughout the United States, Canada and Europe. The subject of countless academic critiques and theses, it has been anthologised in more than one hundred collections. She is a member of Aosdána, the Irish Academy of Writers and Artists and is a Research Associate at Trinity College where for many years she led seminars at the Centre for Gender and Women's Studies. The first Irish woman in history to advocate for LGBT rights, she is a lifelong activist for gay and women's rights. Founder member of 'Irish Women United,' 'The Sexual Liberation Movement,' and 'Women for Radical Change.' Her poetry is taught in schools at O-Level in Britain and on the Irish Junior Certificate. She has lived in England, the USA, France, Japan, Italy and Spain. She has published nine previous books: *Kindling* (Onlywomen Press, 1982); *A Noise from the Woodshed* (Onlywomen Press, 1987); *Moving into the Space Cleared by our Mothers* (Salmon Poetry, 1991); *Scarlet O'Hara* (Onlywomen Press, 1993); *The River that Carries me* (Salmon Poetry, 1995); *Biography of Desire* (Poolbeg, 1997); *Like Joy in Season, like Sorrow* (Salmon Poetry, 2001); *Perhaps the Heart is Constant after All* (Salmon Poetry, 2012); and *To Air the Soul Throw All the Windows Wide: New & Selected Poems* (Salmon Poetry, 2016). She is currently working on a collection of novellas. She lives in Wicklow, Ireland.

ACKNOWLEDGEMENTS

Acknowledgements and my thanks are due to many individuals and institutions who have supported my work in the making of this collection. First in my thoughts is the artist and dear friend, Janet Pierce, who gave me the use of her magnificent painting, *Uisce Anam 'j'*, for my cover.

My gratitude is due also to several national institutions who have honoured my work over the last years: Aosdána, The Museum of Irish Literature (MoLI) The National Library Archive, University College Dublin, Poetry Archive, University College Cork, University College Galway, University College Limerick, Women's History Association of Ireland (WHAI) Dublin Castle, The Department of Culture, Heritage and the Gaeltacht.

I also wish to thank the international scholars, too numerous to name, who have published studies on my writing over the years and the universities where they teach. Many individuals who have published or recorded my poetry, deserve special thanks: Sinéad Gleeson; Éilís Ní Dhuibhne; Noelle Moran and Conor Graham, editors at UCD Press; Patrick McCabe; Nessa O'Mahony; Paul McVeigh; Kathleen Watkins; Dr. Eibhear Walshe; José Carregal-Romero; Dr. Paul D'Alton; Benedict Schlepper-Connolly; Alan Hayes; Dr. Maria Micaela Coppola, University of Trento; Evelyn Conlon; Jean O'Brien; Edmund Lynch; Ruth Lane; Anna Maria Robustelli, La Vita Felice; Dr. Mary McAuliffe; Dr. Aideen Quilty; Dr. Ger Moane; Patrick G. O'Shea, former president UCC; Louise C. Callaghan; A.&A. Farmar; Emma Donoghue; Tony Walshe; Dr. Linda Connolly; Sinead McCoole; Michelle Boyle. Dr. Eimear O'Connor and Dr. Pat Donlon at the Tyrone Guthrie Centre at Annaghmakerrig and Nora Hickey M'Sichili at Le Centre Culturel Irlandais Paris are, respectively, due particular gratitude for sheltering me through several residencies where many of these poems were composed.

Last, but invaluable for their gift of friendship, I wish to thank Irene Brady, Linda Plunkett, Marie Bashford Synnott, Grainne Blair, Elizabeth Greisman, Ailbhe Smyth, Lainey Ennis, Colleen McMahon, Nicola Morrin, Mary Tritschler, and Mary Finn.

Finally, my heartfelt thanks to Jessie Lendennie of Salmon Poetry for her early enthusiasm and continued encouragement of my work and, to Siobhán Hutson of Salmon Poetry for her art work, diligence and patience.

were and are and must always be, the women your
mothers will talk about when they boast that once they
                watched light streeling on a Liffey
                bridge as we besieged the barred
gate of herstory, and they stood against the calumnies

of dusk and raised their voices to cheer our passage.

BANSHEE

We marched through city streets, through the drunken
sprawl of its comedy, the shame tight-nosed, its
          rank respectability, past the hissing
             pulpit, its heavy gang, the twists
and turns of its psyche, in dank alley-ways of history,

the stench of church, of choir and confessional,
along emptied, staring quays, past canopied parliaments
             Georgian gloaming, the last hurrah
             of aristocracy, we hunted the course
of a river still muttering, of cute whores, passivity and

exile, through fuming crowds or crippled statuary, faded
gentility, on nights of sulphur and daylight streams
             we came at last by deliberate surprise
             a hundred years late, all at once, as one,
out into the open, to radiant halls, lush pasture, racing

waters, revelry, the half-remembered sky, of dream, of
love, of literary glory and the first, fine elation, passion
             uncensored, full-throated we cried
             out defiance, banners lifted high to the
lowering cloud, our voices higher, in the rebel's amorous

embrace, pride flared as new, an old euphoria broke
ground, 'Oh sisters don't you weep, don't you mourn.' Our
             lamps torched the air and branded it.
             We are the women our mothers
warned us about. Our bodies ourselves, our words. We

75

INCAUTIOUS PIONEERS

It is a grace we share when together,
the two of us
though we maunder from city to town,

strangers from this place to that
sure-footed as gypsies,
incautious pioneers, waylaid by

ardour, wherever we pitch up, set
camp or make home,
intuition or schemed, back street or

avenue, shadowed or sun-threshed,
no matter how far
we have come, how little familiar,

the secretive hills implacable, the
coastline sensuous,
harrowed by living; it is the same,

unerring, each time between us.
Night or day, the least
friction of nerves, a glance or

meeting of breath, at a touch, the
laws of geography
yield to our sense, there we find

ourselves, waking to one moment.
aboriginals,
arrived at the centre of the world.

Reckless at any rate
it was
of you,
to discount
the season's largesse —
irretrievable favour.

And to scorn —
where paths
diverged at a
shoreline —
the last lover
who will gaze at you
and find
you
beautiful.

WINTER SUNLIGHT

Was it accident or fate
that led us astray —
did I lose my nerve
or you your timing?
Whichever.
Foolish it may have been
to miss the hour
the landmark —

conversation
subtle, quick
in the well established
pattern of years —
to listen
without words
to see by touch .

And afterwards
clustered
in bare arms
crimson petals —
fallen to earth,
a late-flowering
fuchsia.
Had you forgotten?

Were you blinded
by the glare
winter sunlight —
a shaft thrust level
with my shoulder?
Why else
lose your footing
only then?

you liked more than looking at her, not having yet, after nine

years, tired of the mystery of her — the sinuous, exceptional
way her face and body were put together, each separate part,
infused with its own sensuous energy, each part matching
every other and all of it together animated by a spirit more

anarchic than any you had come across before. 'What are

you looking at?' you asked. 'You,' she replied at once. 'In the
whole world there is no one like you.' 'That's exactly what I
was going to say to you,' you said. And the cats yawned
and the fire grew loud against the wind's roar. Your voices

dimmed, you fell back into your books, the dogs dreaming,

the sheep on the mountain-side singing until you bestirred
yourselves, climbed the tall stairs, to the wide gale-tossed bed,
stars dancing in the skylight, the distant sea tumbling on the
sands, you gathered together in four arms and winter sleep.

COUNTRY LIFE

But in the winter her flame was banked down and smouldered

softly. She lay slumberous in the hammock that stretched
across the room from bookshelf to stove where she dozed
like a wintering lion after the labours of summer. She rose
only to cook, for the pleasure it gave her eyes and hands.

She ate sparingly, with less interest than she found in creating

Banquets for her friends to share. Sometimes she gardened
while you were composing in the stripped-down, grass green
caravan. You sat beside the pot-belly stove; the held-breath
of the mountain and lake, sheltering, all about. You recall

Once in a January storm, how she had crawled on hands

and knees across the frozen mud of lazy beds, a scarlet
shawl wrapped about her head, a leather air-force jacket
tied across her back, pellets of snow falling on her eyes and
mouth. It resembled a scene from Siberia — as you imagined

a scene from Siberia must look (thinking of Tolstoy and

Pasternak who nobody thinks of now) a serf toiling across
an ice-ridden plain on some long forgotten Russian plantation.
Afterwards you went indoors, added fuel to the fire and settled
in for the night, with books, animals and wine. 'What are you

looking at?' she queried about an hour onwards, breaking a

soft turf-smoked silence. 'You,' you said after another, not so
long pause. 'Why?' she asked, allowing another interval in
which you heard the purring of the four cats who lay along
side her in the rainbow hewed hammock. There was nothing

ART

Quick as a darting
swift,
bold as the swan's
wing as
she passes
above you,
a boat cleaves —
the lake,
water glistens
from the oar's
blade,
falls
on the still surface,
a spider's web
cast.

5.

Time It Was

To me —
warm air,
closeness,
touch.
Yearning.

LAST SIGHT

As you reached
your lips
to her cheek
you recognised
the serene smile
patient, nostalgic –

The golden light
in her eyes
of the newly-made
soul.
Your nostrils still
full with the fragrance

Of death
you saw that she
was attending –
entirely composed
for an unseen
arrival.

Listening with
practised
confidence
for the songs
of the dead –

Gathered,
so many,
so fond
at her shoulder.
Come back

singing old songs no one recalls, urging
forgotten choirs
to lift their voice, to keep a watchful
eye, on the tardy,
the apostate, the blithe revellers above
ground. To listen for
the footstep, to set a votive flame –
to prepare the way.

LAST RITES

Even now, in this house of last rites —
you are kneeling
in the church where they carried me
for baptism and
led me by the hand to make a first
communion. Under
the same rafters
in that very year, my father slept his

ultimate night above earth. Can it be
wondered then
as I wait for your return, the beating
of wings at my
back, the clouds hushed, as I labour,
breaking stones
in the yard of
unrepentant sentence that I find

myself instead, writing letters to the
angels, enjoining them to
keep a heedful ear, the hearth swept
clear, asking that they
remember irretrievable time, rooms
loud with gaiety,
contention,
inspiration; two people young, the

years and love crowding about them,
skies stretching
endless in front. And so, picturing you
in that chapel
at prayer, under the same roof where
my mother
and father lay
forty years apart, what wonder if I am

LOSS

Setting off once more —
the old track
downhill, racing
past the great oak
the boat house,
hastening towards the

final curve of the path,
my blood stirs:
Be quiet childish heart,
remember —
everything passes,
every branch breaks.

And sure enough
this moment —
turning the home bend
of the road —
only one dog comes
ambling
to greet me
at the gate.

GONE

A deserted stage —
slighted, idle.

Its hands chill
mouth vacant.

Air stiff
at the window,

furniture rebuffed.
Set and costumes

abandoned,
pattern without

purpose.
A bed holds your

imprint still —
tea cold in a flowered cup.

If this were all I knew
of life,
if it were all I was to learn —
of trial,
of reclamation

then, hearing this
seeing you thus —
faltering step
knuckles gripping
white —

it would be enough
to comprehend
all wisdom
of the sages.
All serenity.
All loss.

* from "Finis Exoptatus"
  by Adam Lindsay Gordon,
  1833–1870

GRIPPING THE BANNISTER

You made your way
towards me
fearful
intrepid,
clutching the bannister
in your last abode.

Graven face
hand over hand,
I came upon you
by surprise —
you, repeating

in subterranean,
urgent tones,
a verse
retrieved from
the once
lustrous
caverns of childhood.

one word enunciated
with each
deliberate step:
'Life, is mostly
froth and bubble.
Two things stand
like stone:
compassion in another's
trouble,
courage in one's own." *

DECEMBER LIGHT

At the stone rim of the year
earth holds her breath.
December light labours

from a sky of foil,
all that happened was this —
an old woman

walking an old dog:
we stopped to talk
a moment.

'She's a darling,' I said
you're a great pair.
Which leading the other?'

and they smiled at me
both, the dog
and her faithful companion.

I reach my heart
to these small encounters
as you might warm

your hands at
a street brazier
on a winter's day.

4.
Trial and Reclamation

rain, starlings taking
flight into a golden evening.
You are turning her into a movie:
the figure of a woman poised on a
granite step, a silk shawl drawn at her
shoulder. You will catch the final scene

as the limousine
bears you down an avenue
of laurel, as the house turns its
back on the last of august. 'I thought
nothing of her when we met.' Already
you see the bitter alchemy take hold –

the radiant, aching
present that engulfs
this instant will glide on silent
tracks, as now you wish it could,
beyond vigilance, beyond sound or view,
into the eternal, the mired, irretrievable, then.

A LAST GLIMPSE OF SUMMER

You must make her into a story you
are telling a new woman, an
elegant, discerning woman,
living in a foreign town.
You are drinking Pastis
together, lolling

by the Seine, you run through the
inventory of profit and loss,
'There was one,' you will
say, 'who almost broke
my heart.' You are
making her into a

story. Images you can stop and start,
excise or embroider. You see the
new woman's face, vivid
with sympathy, longing.
You describe the scene,
already as if snatched

from a train window, the fields, the
woods, the lake, ebbing from your
gaze. 'She was older than me.'
you will say: 'I thought
nothing of her when
we met and yet…'

There will be a last glimpse of summer

every faith else was sundered and lost. Then gusts of beauty

despite all, small squalls of joy when least expected came

blowing in without warning, startling me back to connection
when almost forgotten when all almost foundered. I walk now
on this hard, shifting bridge two inches clear of perdition, one

step at a time, eyes down patient for restoration, or a staff to

bear me, sturdy as oak, honest and plain as weathered boots
to carry me out of the mire back to communion
and light. Only a poem, a good one will do.

THE NARROW TRACK, GRIEF

I walk on the swaying timber of this perilous
pontoon bridge, two inches clear of the mire. I need a
a poem, only a poem, a good one will do; a staff to bear me;

sturdy, honest as wood to carry me from this morass, only

a poem, a good one will do. Beauty to all sides and grace on
this stony, comfortless path. The animals leap in the fields,
the water runs orange and brash, its noisy spring choir, the

lash of its voice, old habits reviving, nature in transport all

round me; from mountains cascading, rising from bogland
spring birds cantering, fallow deer singing while the skies
wheel in glory, the sun basks in its power chanting the

pristine clear music of light returning. And hunger for touch

revives as each living thing reaches out, trembling with
new perception, each sensate creature avid for life, hungry
to start the race of continuation. I walk on the tremulous

timber of this perilous pontoon bridge, two inches clear

of the slough, my eyes on the ground silent and silenced. I
trudge without words, without even their memory, stripped
of delusion of new commencement though all of creation

bellows its faith in rebirth as though it were easy. Spring.

I walk muted, eyes down without even the solace of cadence
and image, only the memory of a time before remains when

Who thieves
with amorous flattery.
Who can we ask
to unearth it;
ancient bone

From the fen,
brittle, porous, a relic,
study, cleanse it,
hew and polish it
until smoothed

Fine as crystal,
so keen
even the most skilled
among them:
the autocrat,
the publicist,
the treacherous lover,

The poet —
hesitates
to loose it
from the tongue —
lest they cut their lip
on the whetted

Edge
of
one,
stripped,
lucid,
heart-driven
word.

WORDS

Somebody has to do it —
plead for the word,
labour for it.
Retrieve it
from the grime
of daily usage,

Trampled by
hypocrisy;
the saccharine lie
of buying and selling,
of politics and war.
Prise it

From the hypocrite,
the cowardice
of the comfortable;
embezzlement
by priests and princes
who camouflage

Diktat with
the chrism of piety.
Somebody must,
release the word
from the greased palm
of the world,

From the huckster
and the fraud,
from the mouth of
blandishment,
false promise;
the eyes of the beloved

swathe of gold and silver astonishes the grass, its taste
and scent seductive
as the bumble bee's flight. A birch tree shoots from a

crimson river, colour strikes the canvas quivering; with
a sound like snow
on falling leaves. Where is it bound? What is it for? Is

it the artisan's intention that pre-occupies the cat, or
is the mystery
of memory the hook of her attention? From where

does it derive the original spur of plot and theme
both players seem to ask.
Can this ever be foreseen or even understood? If I

dear cat, I would know more than the painter knows who
knows much less than
you, who knows much more than me. And if paint were

words and cats could sing and the melody of startled
birds could teach a cat
to laugh or show a painter how to dance then perhaps

when I invent these reasons and their rhymes, it may
seem I am become
poor poet, all three of these at last: painter, paint and cat.

THE PAINTER'S CAT

I want to be the painter's cat, watching from the table by
the painter's easel,
could I share her rapt attention. It is not the soft descent

of a winding sea-green line, alone that fascinates this cat
who loves all rippling
things: a falling stone, a shaken rose, a spider crawling.

Rain. But something else is here, I spy, while her gleaming
gaze trails the
scented paint, its serpentine coil mesmeric. The artist's

hand purrs softly as it glides along the page, a rainbow
sudden in a yellow sky
sets the cat's tail throbbing; the brush moves onwards,

a horse rears up, the secret engine in the feline's throat
begins its own
percussion. Does the dazzlement of senses pleasure

cat as much as painter, or could it be the artistic plan
that captivates the feline
mind? The brush slips downwards, a house begins to

canter, a frog leaps from the painter's thumb, the cat's
head darts
to catch whatever may spring next from this seductive

mouse-hole. The human watches the colour move, the
cat courts the odyssey,
one paw lifted to ravish any trickery of fleeting light. A

46

I am driven like a donkey
by my gift along
hard roads and soft –
goaded by the whip
enticed by
a sheaf of straw.

Striving with half a mind
to succeed at
ordinary things.
Never arriving –
forever
reaching.

BETWEEN THE SHAFTS

I am driven like a donkey
by my gift —
uphill and down,
along rough roads and soft,
striving with half a will
to succeed
at ordinary things —
always failing.

Drawn like a mule
hoof after head,
along iron tracks
in winter, stumbling on
the cobble stones,
tumbling into ditches.
On the cliff edge
by night, throat
parched, voiceless.

Sometimes,
at the season's turn,
by a wild
mountain stream
bathing,
or it might be at dawn
breaking into song.

On occasion,
perhaps,
getting up a canter,
at others,
a bright wind
at my back —
flying a few feet
above the crowd.

COMMON QUESTIONS AND SOME ANSWERS

They asked her if she had children. They asked
her why not. They asked her if she had ever
wanted children. Why not they asked. You would

have made a wonderful mother, they said. But
what was that, she queried. She had never met
a woman who described herself as such or knew

what it would look like, to be a wonderful mother.
But isn't it selfish, they said. What? she asked. Not
to have any, they said. Why? she asked. Because,

They said, we all have to do our bit – to make a
contribution. To make more people? she said. Yes,
they replied. To make people, to look after other

people? she asked, who will make more people? Yes,
they answered. That's it. To be unselfish, they said.
Well, she considered for a moment. If I had ever

noticed an under-supply of people, she said. I might
have felt the same. I might have felt I ought to do my
bit, to manufacture other people. But in the second

half of the twentieth century, I saw not the slightest
shortage of other human beings. There was, however,
a severe drought of poets. Especially, she said, of

women poets. So I thought I should put my shoulder
to the wheel, make a contribution. Be unselfish. Add
one more woman to their number. And even now, she

said, forty years later there are still more babies, it
seems to me, than poets. And more women making
them. Than poets. Especially, she said, women poets.

3.

The Artist's Road

scream broke through her terror? When he forced the
blindfold on, the handcuffs and the gag? How could
she defend herself? How would you have broken

free? Or anyone of us? Hunted, bound and blinded,

driven fifty miles from home. How she struggled. How
she swore. But how could anyone have heard ? How
could any eye see when at last he threw her out, in

the silent, secret dark. He found it so exciting to

watch her final panic, her begging and her fear, so
he dragged her to a wood, raped her, strangled her.
And burnt her to the bone. Just like you. Just like me.

She was only walking home, leaving the light

of a cafe and a friend. As if she had the right as if
she were free to walk the streets at night. Why do
men hate us, so much they hunt and kill us? Why

do they not ask themselves until it's too late? Is

jealousy or fear of life their goad? Do they blame us
women for bearing them? Or is the crime they can't
forgive, the original sin —
that first expulsion
from the womb?

EDEN

She was only
walking home.
Just like you. Just like me.

Leaving the light of a cafe and a friend. As if she had
the right, as if she were free to walk the streets at night.
She was only walking home. At night in the dark. She

trusted a man, an officer in blue watching out for her

Wouldn't I? Wouldn't you? When you're only walking
home? It could have been me. It could have been you,
trusting a friendly Bobby in Blue. Offering assistance

'Just to see you safe love. Just to get you home.' Alone

in the dark. Her own front door, half a mile away.
How could she have known? Why would she suspect?
Why would you have realised? Or anyone of us? No

thank you, she said 'I'm good as I am. Just leaving a

friend. On my way home.' Why would she have worried
how would you have guessed; a smiling man in uniform,
offering advice. Alone in the dark, his hand on her arm

explaining how dangerous to stay out late it was. How

soon did she begin to doubt ? How soon would you
have worked it out? Should she have guessed? Would
I have known? Just before he slammed the door and

locked the windows shut? How long before the first

She carry it off, spurn the come-ons, the put-downs, the
leers, the bribes, the bait,
the sweeteners, the ribbons and roses, the grip of the

Tightening choker? For how much longer hold back the
claque in the front stalls, the bosses, the
coked-up, the pimps, the cat-calls, the slow hand-clapping,

The throats salivating. And that stare, that razor-cold eye –
get it off, they cheer from the
gallery, get them off you, daring her to shed, to the last stitch,

Her silk, her furs, her leathers, her diamond ring, her string
of pearl, each bud that still clings,
each leaf and flower stripped for the profit. Give it over to us

Girl, give it over, they jeer, avid to tear meat from bone, to
eat her all up, every delicate
shred, each gob-full, to the final raw-red, pound of her earth.

PREDATION OF EARTH

The trees parade October bloom, their classic chic, once
again dazzling in matched amber and gold.
The river is babbling, yes, that exact cliche, pure autumn

Notes, white frothed glee, pitch perfect, its revival of cast
and season. The clouds hang calm,
inquisitive, to eavesdrop on the confabulation of crows,

Who bow, shift and scatter, black-tasseled fright and high
chatter over newly shorn fields.
These old urgencies, year after year, messages inscribed

On thin air, the same glory wide and near, the same gilded
trick nature in rapture slips from
her sleeve, as though it could go on unceasing, as if never

To count the cost. But, does she yet, sense the quickening
breath, mark rehearsal time
grow shorter, in these extravagant, spendthrift days of fall?

For how much longer can she pull it off, this vintage routine
– stripping ageing limbs
nude, free of charge for the herd? Each season the same

Break-neck pace, this quick-change artistry, the same
promise offered, the same largesse.
How many more times can she work the crowd, for a pack,

Grown gluttonous, flesh fed, weary of marvel: how she
makes easy each day, her slight of
hand miracle: dark into light. How many more times can

Excelsis Deo: does it soften the blow, you ask
or whet the blade in this
landscape of loss perpetual, the wind exiled

to some other pastoral, the rain
dumb, the valley sightless, what does it signify,
this pallid grist of private sorrow?

You will not hear her voice again.

ANOTHER PASTORAL

December morning splendour, sheer as an axe —
            in the last days falling —
trees freighted green still, a stripped sky

               bare of cloud,
the wind banished to some other country.
            Radiance streams from

heaven afar, while the world gets on with its
              practiced horrors —
slaughter and those fond attendants, hunger

             rapine, torture. From
sea to sea, anguish girds the sensate earth
            street and field torched

by gorgeous flame, men must have a trade
             or some show of
occupation and their loyal apostles must

            record in word and icon the
yearly ration of obscenity. Silent night, holy night;
            in the final month, heavenly

hosts raise their voice as if hymns of praise
             might yet cast the balm of
history across the pillaged clay while winter

            sunlight spills its glory on the gouged
faces, the gaily coloured debris, the stench of
            burning children. Gloria in

Watchful
smile,
a hand
lifted to her throat –
a creature half-tamed,
alarmed by sudden
light, startled and at bay.

ALARMED BY SUDDEN WARNING

There was talk of danger,
of violence and threat,
you held her gaze —
a nocturnal creature
huddled in a dim lair —
a half-made bed
piled high with
cushions.

You offered solemn
phrases —
explanation and
good council
but all you saw
was the
sensual curve
of her hip

Beneath the skirt
of black velvet
and the muted
oyster-blue
of her eyes
reflecting yours.
From a doused

Flame
a spark blew up
sudden —
as fear or desire
between you,
you saw again
in the swift

The brook, chasing, falling, maternal cries chiding, clear as
a choir of starlings. What are they thinking? What are they dreaming,
these mothers, their off-spring, a meandering
home-coming, what do they see that I cannot?
All this buoyancy, fervour and grace is elusive, ephemeral, imperilled.
Why is my heart rioting? I get out early in winter to see the world.

To set the blood stirring.

motion of clouds suffuses my gaze, how they sail and
settle, their surge and retreat like waves gust-blown to harbour in
childhood: romance and revolt at a bedroom
window, the roar and sigh, riot and shelter, the
ocean still, in my ear, each morning on waking. I get out later in
winter to see the world. Old men walk trembling, beating a path

with their sticks, canines tail chasing, fetch the end of
each circle, losing their start. A young woman approachs from her
sleeve a child trailing. What happened, I ask, seeing
the muddy tears, "She slipped at the gate
coming out from class, running to meet me, fell on the mucky
path and look, ruined her coat and her knees.' How fortunate,

having a mother to run to, I say. They stare at me both
with alarm, then together accept to decide it as kind. I get out later
in winter to see the world. Good will and
seasonal beauty, laud the scene, ribbons
of light in valley and hill, a song-burst of sparrows from an ivy bush
and the giddy chit-chat, small persons, a wandering rivulet home-

coming, rivals the crows: their thoughts slick in mackintosh
feathers, bead-blue eyes quick as the childish larking. What do they know
that I cannot? What do they see? Always the
same, delight and hatred, rage and beauty
hand in glove. Joy and shame. Rivers of war flow now here, now there
from this village to that, earth-flooded, beast-starved and meanwhile

on the far side of the street, light persuasive as melody
orders the clouds, lovers confide in the long grass languid. What do
they know that I cannot? What do they hear?
A fanfare of doves conducts the air, rooks with
their black semaphore, croak-croaking, thorn-crowned goats out-
pace the hare, canter down-hill, as the kids home coming out-talk

IN DAYS OF CONTAGION

I get out early in winter to see the world
to set the blood stirring. Good will and seasonal beauty
        varnish the air, sunlight snared like vine
        on the horns of mountainy sheep, over
field and hill a cloud burst of starlings, while lovers wrangle in
hedgerow and lane, crows in conspiracy, caw-calling, rival

        The giddy chif-chaf of school children home
coming, a stream meandering, supple and hardy as raven
        oak in December. I get out early and late
        in winter to see the world, to set the blood
stirring. Decay and debris, rubbish and grief are evenly spread
in contagious season, abandoned waste tossed off by the wind,

        Paper cups, under-pants, boots and sheets,
the world elsewhere goes on as always usual, rivers of war
        flood now there, now here, not the first nor
        the last, these have no number, they ravage
unchanging from that village to this, earth starved, beasts
broken, women and children burnt to death in flaming streets.

        Nowhere to run. Nobody cares. What can you
do? Turn off the tv. I think of them as I walk, the babies, the
        bombs. I think of them. I get out early
        in winter to see the world. A friend, I learn is
grievously ill and yesterday morning the love of her life died
without warning. The pain of her pain sears my chest. I have

        few words of solace, scarce enough for myself.
I get out later in winter to see the world, ribbons of sunlight hang
        in low branches as tailing each other, a skirmish
        of squirrels haul chestnuts on high, always
the same; horror and glory, cheek by jowl, rage and beauty,
street by street, torture and joy. I lift my face to the sky, the

2.
Life Holds Its Breath

There might be wine or not.
A magpie comes to clean her
feathers in the smoke rising
from the chimney top.
I hear her singing.

If there's something
on the box we both like
we might watch it.
We could listen to a
favourite piece of music,
we might dance or not.
Afterwards
in the quiet when birds sleep,
and a yellow moon lolls against

The mountain's shoulder, we talk
about the afternoon, you recall
the river, the way it hurls
itself headlong over every obstacle,
undaunted. I remember
the beginning of the day,
drinking coffee out in the open,
the early sun dancing in your eyes,

So that I remarked again how blue
they are, knowing
in fact they are green, pale as
first leaf in spring.
Though to me
in one mood or attitude
they seem a rare
blue, promising as limpid sky,
cloudless, at the start of the day.

'Exactly,' you reply.
At other times we sit by the bank,
there is often a bench
or a smooth rock. We
gaze at the stream that is ruby
red, the way sunlight
escapes from a passing cloud
to fall precisely on one
burnished flank that
describes
the whole lithe length of it.

'As you would paint it,' you say
'if you were to paint it.'
We talk about the everyday
things, the week gone by,
comical moments, a transient
worry solved, a happy surprise,
Some wounding that happened
to a friend.

I take your hand between mine,
the slender bones,
unblemished skin, soft
as down. As eider-down
is said to be.
I sit without words.
So glad in that moment to be
in our lives and not some other.

We get home around six
usually. Not too
late to make dinner.
We might light a fire
of wood or turf.

A pheasant, I suggest
In danger? you ask
I wouldn't think so —
more likely a male
showing off new attire.
Country customs, you say
Now, you have it, I reply.

There is usually,
a river, classical
serpentine, flaunting it's
luxurious way around rock
and bank,
tossing a rust-white
mane in triumph over each
impediment —
polished stone or timber.

Coal black, three young sheep
stare from a five-barred gate.
I watch them watching us
with their enquiring,
tender regard.
You are explaining to me
the theological
distinction between hope
and optimism.
It has occupied you for
some while.
'We must first know despair,' I say
'to understand hope.'

MOST DAYS

Most days begin in the same way —
drinking strong coffee,
facing the sun.
We might be reading books
or maybe not.
I say how blue your eyes are
in strong light,
you remind me they are green.

Afterwards, unless the rain is
heavy, we walk.
The place is almost always
the same,
though in different locations.
More often than not
there's an avenue —
high trees, story-book boughs

Heavy with bloom, by times
yellow or red,
at others emerald, allowing
for the month of year.
They reach sinuous arms
across a wide driveway —
to greet kinsfolk
on the far side.

From the forest, all at once
quite often, comes
a sudden shriek, high-pitched
dramatic
it startles you each time.
There it goes again, you say,
that noise.

IN MY HOUSE

Mornings
when
through the glass pane
glancing in —
to find you sleeping,
still —
in my house,
safe —
summer warmth
burnishes
the dust-lined
chambers
of thought,
clear
as august
colour
blooming
in the chill
air
of a winter
season.

AFTER RAIN

Stillness
of winter,
sleeping light —
the wind's breath
held,

I like to talk
with you,

the birch
and the oak
lost in thought,
gaze
crest-fallen,

I like to look
at you,

small birds
harvest news,
flight
close-folded,
a low sun

observes the
scene —
drenches
the leaves
with gold,

I like to touch you.

WHAT WE TAKE AS GRACE

Is this then, the composition of what we take as grace,
its denotation? An advent we can
neither summon nor refuse? Was there something of this
nature in the manner of our
meeting though quiet, unremarkable that first attaching of

Our lives? Coming at the least predicted hour, we might
each have overlooked the other,
nothing in the name, the hue of weather or the number of
the day alerting us. But standing
at the centre of a room, in a ring of noisy strangers, a turn

Of pace or energy, and people all about began to dance.
Left close, unattended, we sat down
together by an open door and talked. We did not look one
at the other, only ahead at
the people passing in the loudness all around. Was it there,

In that half-attention, it reached me without prelude, in a
soft, sudden, inner shift, the least
movement, scarcely felt, just beneath the heart? Was this
presentiment, the sensing
of an element, impervious to time? A cast of mind, a

disposition forged in stillness? A way of being, a woman I
could trust? In that split-moment
had I glimpsed a forgotten gift? That I was speaking as
if you understood my words, that
you were listening as though I recognised your thoughts.

THE FORGOTTEN GIFT

Is this how we recognise it?
Is it the nature and
definition

Of the thing, arriving without preamble, unannounced, the
setting unfamiliar; the last place we might have thought to
seek? At others, is it the timing that takes us unawares,

The aghast, sheer blue of it, a lightening bolt rending a night-
time sea? In another element we might find it, the first
bloom torn from a branch in April storm, lifting it from our

Path, we inhale the variegated scent, had we forgotten this
perfection; the colours brilliantly mismatched, the skin's
voluptuous satin, vulnerable as if it were the original of

The species, just made. Or in a different season, could it
arrive as music unattended, its enchantment escaping
from behind a bolted door, a forgotten chapel, a city

Street, we stand struck-still, compelled to listen. We
cannot name the piece but it recovers us, each plangent
motion of the bow, unbidden, tempers blood and memory.

As if the earth itself might give voice to joy,
might orchestrate its
sorrows.

all of a sudden, without presage or fore-
cast, from the maelstrom snatched: a
shadow or manner of walking, a shift of
the head, some impulse of delight that

previsioned an element of you. So tell me,
if anyone will because I cannot, why this
should happen, often or ever? Whether

strolling alone in an alien village or city,
linked arm in arm with some companion
beloved, high on late night confabulations,
in any random, unchosen place without

warning or seeking, as I strayed up or down
some thronged boulevard where all the world:
one thousand, ten thousand lives or more

coursed by, without record, unremarked in
the tide, unreasoning flood, humanity un-
stoppable. Why then, seldom but some times
by what cause or what purpose, one gaze

from the mill escapes; one unknown pair
of eyes grasps mine, a glance that strikes
home, swift as the point of a blade, its

impact registered in mind and blood, as
it pierces flesh and lodges. Tell me why
if you could, it should happen this way? Tell
me, you. My last love, because I cannot.

IF OUR PATHS WERE TO CROSS

Would I know you at once, for certain, you
my last love, if our paths were to cross by
chance, after all, how many years can it be

since I filched even a trace of your features
in the crowd? Questions unanswered assail
me: what would you look like these days,
how do you live, alone or with others, what

work sustains you? Is it a passion or drudge?
Would you do it for pleasure if nobody
thanked or paid you? Are you romantic

by nature or worldly? What at this stage, do
you believe about love? What terms have
you found to accommodate death? You see,
I know nothing the heart yearns to know

and brought to hard facts, even less can
I claim. Not least where you grew up or
were born. Nor even what country or city

now owns you. It might as well be Bagdad,
as Bologna or Boston. I've passed through
all these and more, found friends; wild times
and luminous but no face more lasting than

might be surprised at an airport gangway or
any misplaced country station. Mere marks
on the compass in each but one. Yet there,

at once the thing itself and their symbol,
arrived now
before your startled gaze, apparel at
least, an
echo from a past familiar; a command

performance your senses studied to
recognise
as fate. The orchestra waits, the fire-
curtain up, a
visiting conductor adjusts coat-tails in

the wings, the audience is hushed, feet
stilled. The first
violin draws her bow, that plaintive note,
at once recalled,
a tremor passes through the crowd,

pity, longing, hope, vie for orchestration
in their breath.
Coiffure and evening dress precisely in
place; reason
rivals blood in their staggered pulse.

REASON RIVALS BLOOD

Youth come again and summer, honeyed
light, fragrant ground,
everything new, as of old, starting out,
wide eyed, the self yields
once more to story, a novel thrown open,

binding freshly stitched, that inhalation
recalled,
leaves uncut. Reverie seeks for signals
in chapter
headings: obsession, affection, desire,

these neglected characters sound from
off-field, prick the
hearing, cause the heart to stammer.
Words will not help,
their fluency deserts you, they stumble

from the lips, edges blurred, their rhythm
jagged as your
breathing. A novice once more, setting
off, interpretation
untried, a classic role, script and lighting

in rehearsal, stage-craft uncertain, even
to a practised
hand, clumsy, unpredictable. An image,
a voice, a touch
have taken centre stage, these heralds,

Memory holds
us captive,
companions in
love and grief,
we read them
in the secret text
of our blood.

The heart is like that.

THE HEART IS LIKE THAT

Without permission
people inscribe
themselves on it
at our birth
or theirs
or long before.
Concealed,

They lurk, hidden
in the cellular
code to be
read at a future
place or period.
Intimates from

A former life, found
or mislaid, their
world
forgotten, yet
we know them
at the touch

Of a voice,
at first glance wherever
they discover us.
Dream-like, mythical,
entirely familiar
we have no shield —

When high on the bough
we grasp it
or caught in surprise —
find it
tumbled into our lap.

Prize it wherever it seeds,
from whichever eyes

Deserving or not it
may gleam.
Speak of it
softly, touch it with
the hands of a lover.

Set it on newly-mown grass
in the sun, a white cloth spread —

Air the wine.
Inhale this moment,
its taste
like love —
the bloom still ripe
on its skin.

DO NOT COUNT THE HOURS

Do not envy
another's content
whoever may own it,
a long or brief
sojourn in pleasure –
its stillness
its light.

Do not resent however it comes,
another's display of good fortune

Though it circles them –
a halo of ease,
a blindfold of riches.
Happiness in any soil
whatever year,

Is perishable fruit, bruised by the
weight of a kiss as swiftly as greed,

Undefended
against age, poverty,
weather,
frayed
by caprice –
the contradictions
of the heart.

Do not count the hours
or wish for another season

1.
*Youth Come Again
And Summer*

4. *Trial and Reclamation*

December Light	57
Gripping the Bannister	58
Gone	60
Loss	61
Last Rites	62
Last Sight	64

5. *Time It Was*

Art	69
Country Life	70
Winter Sunlight	72
Incautious Pioneers	74
Banshee	75

Acknowledgements	78
About the Author	80